Serenity in Your Space:

How I Found Mine

Copyright © 2022 by Donna L. Dunn

All rights reserved.

No portion of this book may be reproduced in any form without written permission from the publisher or author, except as permitted by U.S. copyright law.

Published by Diane Novack

Cover design by Shanna Sites

Table of Contents

Introduction 6

Dedication 8

Thank you 11

Review of: Serenity in Your Space, How I Found

Mine 15

Chapter 1 24

Who Am I ? 24

    HELPFUL TIPS 38

Chapter 2 47

Thinking Outside the Box 47

HELPFUL TIPS	57
Chapter 3	*67*
Wow – NOT What I Planned!	*67*
HELPFUL TIPS	99
Chapter 4	*104*
New Life	*104*
Helpful Tips	118
Chapter 5	*126*
Finding a Career	*126*
Helpful Tips	134
Chapter 6	*142*
Being a Teacher	*142*

    Helpful Tips 147

Chapter 7 152

Fixer-Upper 152

    Helpful Tips 161

Chapter 8 168

Letting Go 168

    Helpful Tips 175

Chapter 9 185

New Life Path 185

    Helpful Tips 210

Chapter 10 218

Starting a Business 218

Helpful Tips..224

Chapter 11 232

Coming Out of My Shell 232

Helpful Tips..238

Chapter 12 254

Networking..254

Helpful Tips..272

Chapter 13 286

My Dream 286

Introduction

I wrote this book to share my passion and explain why I left teaching to open up my own business. I had to overcome many struggles and self-doubt to find my peace and serenity. Through telling my story, I will be taking you on a journey where I hope you see how females can be strong, inspiring, and empowered. I pray you are entertained and educated on how you too can find your peace and serenity.

Dedication

This book is dedicated to my two daughters Dana Marie Coons and Kelli Elizabeth Dunn. I am extremely proud of both of you for all you have overcome in your lives. I thank you for encouraging me to follow my dream and take a huge leap of faith. Thank you for being my tech support, cheerleaders, sounding boards, "clients", and best friends. If it was not for you two girls, I would never have survived the loss of your father. You were the reason I got up each day and powered through. Your Dad has never left us and seeing him constantly through your voices, actions, memories and even the wonderful men you choose to love has been a blessing to me. I love you both from the bottom of my heart.

I would also like to dedicate this book to my siblings, Alaina, Chuck, Colleen, Andrew and Curtis, who made growing up in our family so much fun and entertaining. You all

helped me through the worst parts of

my life and love you so much.

Thank you

I would like to thank two special ladies who believed I needed to write this book and tell my story. First, Karen Joseph, my sweet "boss" at SEVEN Networking for believing in me and encouraging me with those gentle pushes to get out of my comfort zone and stretch my wings. Without your constant encouragement and guidance I doubt

I would have made my business last through the pandemic. Your leadership in running SEVEN Networking and all the different topics you gave us to stretch our networking abilities even from our own living rooms was amazing. I learned to do videos, Facebook Lives, Instagram, zoom and even blitzer. Thank you for being my mentor and friend.

Second, I would like to thank Alicia Shumaker. She was a friend I found through SEVEN Networking who ran a chapter in Michigan. Alicia encouraged me to really think about my business and what my why was. She helped me to rebrand my business and to find my inner voice. One conversation with Alicia led me to really think about writing this book that Karen had been "pushing". The next day I sat in my backyard and wrote it from beginning to end. Alicia, thank you for listening to me and helping me find my voice. You made me believe I had a story to tell.

Review of: Serenity in Your Space, How I Found Mine

This book written by author, Donna L. Dunn, *is* an inspirational, easy-read book that I couldn't put down. Donna titles herself as a woman, mother, widow, cancer survivor, former teacher, best-selling author, and an entrepreneur. As I turned the last page, I can confirm she is all that and more.

I am drawn to books written by authors revealing their real-life stories. I love their tales of challenge and how they survive, how they have this deep-rooted belief in themselves, their passions and faith and somehow, as they travel through their maze of life, they find that path that pulls their destiny together.

Donna does all of that within her chapters taking you back to her childhood days, through her marriage to the love of her life, how they both battled cancer together and the heartbreak of losing him. Yet, his tragic loss, gave her the strength to heal and go on to raise her two gifted daughters as a single mom. She heard her voice and desire to teach, finding her way to the hearts of children in her classrooms. Another guidance led her to a path that shared her words by collaborating with other writers that became a best-selling book and then a whole new direction after retirement, starting her own business, *Donna's A Place For Everything,* a successful service to help de-clutter and organize the lives of others.

As you read her life story, the pages are filled with various inspirational quotes that capture the theme of each chapter along with tips on helping you tackle your cluttered spaces that got me excited to try

as they seem so doable.

But what I love most about Donna's book,

are her beliefs you find hidden between

her lines. She, herself, is an open book,

sharing so much of her life. As you read,

you discover this beautiful soul, who has

had her challenges, lived through them,

believed in herself and her faith, and

believes in you by sharing her gifts of

serenity and peace in so many ways to all

of her readers.

Lainie Belcastro, Author, Poet, and Storyteller

Serenity Spot:

The place in your home that calls to you and draws you in, where you feel most comfortable to Stop, Breathe, and Relax.

"Believe you can and you're halfway there."

-Theodore Roosevelt

Chapter 1

Who Am I ?

Although I turned 62 this year, I feel as if I am being reborn and starting life anew. I ask myself, "Who am I? For what do I want to be remembered? What is my passion, my purpose?" I am a: woman; mother; widow; cancer survivor; former teacher; best-selling author and an entrepreneur. My passion is helping people find peace and serenity in their living/working spaces, and in their lives. I help them conquer the feelings of stress and overwhelm –and the often ensuing anxiety– when spaces are cluttered and disorganized. Whether downsizing for their golden years, changing life circumstances, or packing/unpacking to move to a new home, my great desire is helping clients ease into these transitions efficiently and calmly, with joy and optimism for the future.

To understand my perspective, let me take you on a journey of my life up to this point. I am the fourth child in a line of six children born in the 1950s and 1960s. Money was tight, and our parents raised us to appreciate everything we had. One of the fondest memories of my Dad is how he used duct tape as a fix for nearly anything. Seeing him jerry-rig something –and he usually did– before purchasing new, taught me to think outside-the-box and try to repair before spending money unnecessarily. Of course, duct tape has been my longtime friend.

I learned to upcycle by watching my parents reuse things in many different ways. Foil pans went to the garage to corral items for my Dad. Shoeboxes became shelf organizers. Glass spaghetti sauce jars were used to mix ingredients. Long before it became a trend, so many discardable things were repurposed in our home. A few family jokes: "Don't throw away that paper plate— Mommy will wash it!" "Don't crumple that tin foil— it can be reused." "Don't tear the wrapping paper— Mommy will remove the tape and reuse it over... and over... and over again." On a funny note, sometimes our Christmas presents were wrapped in newspaper comics; we saw it as an added treat. As you can probably tell, funds did not flow for frivolous items. I learned at a young age how money could be stretched!

Growing up, I shared a room with my older sister, and she was my best friend. I can laugh about it now, but on Saturday, which were cleaning days, if her things were on my side of the room or if I felt she was taking too long to clean, sometimes I would get frustrated to the point of throwing her stuff outside our bedroom door. That worked for me because the door was on my side. I'm not sure this made her love me more.

Growing up with constant lessons of economizing and not being wasteful served me well when I married and started my own family.

My late husband Michael and I spent nine years trying to buy a house. Ultimately, we had to leave our home state of New Jersey and move to Pennsylvania to accomplish our goal. We bought our house intending to work on it together, as it was definitely a fixer-upper. A Cape Cod-style with two bedrooms, one small bath, living room and tiny kitchen, it also had an attic and cinder block basement– the latter two spaces completely unfinished. Now I realize this seems impossibly small, but considering we had spent the previous five years occupying just two bedrooms and half of the family room at my parents' house, we were in heaven!

Why had we lived with my parents for five years? Having rented an apartment the first three years of our married life, we had not been able to save enough for a down payment on a home. Mom and Dad wanted to buy a condo "down the shore" to enjoy quality time together. My youngest brother was still at home attending high school. So we made an agreement for Michael and I to move in for a year or two, allowing us to build our nest egg, and watching over my youngest brother on the weekends when my parents went to the shore house.

In July 1984, during the first year we lived with them, I gave birth to Dana. Just 10 short months later my mother passed away from injuries/complications sustained in a car accident a few days before. I was 25 years old when this major life event occurred. Talk about a shocking turn of events— from the joy of first-time motherhood to the grief of losing my own mother so suddenly.

My Dad was overwhelmed. He and Mom were truly best friends and partners in every aspect of their lives. Michael and I willingly extended our stay to help my Dad cope. The one or two year plan stretched to five years, and our second daughter, Kelli, was born in March 1989. Four months later we found our first home as a family.

Once we began our new life in Pennsylvania, I had to call upon all my creativity to furnish and decorate it. Thankfully my parents had laid down that solid foundation for thinking outside the box.

"Don't agonize,

ORGANIZE!"

-Florence Kennedy

HELPFUL TIPS

- Feeling Overwhelmed?

Step 1: Take a deep breath, figure out which room contains your "Serenity Spot"– the place in your home that calls to you and draws you in, where you feel most comfortable to Stop, Breathe, and Relax. It's the space which allows you to unwind, center or think things through when you're feeling overwhelmed.

Step 2: Now break it down even further; pick just one section of that room/space and start there.

Step 3: Remove everything from the area, and decide if you need it, if you want it, and evaluate its condition.

Step 4: Return to the space only those items which make sense and are organized for your needs.

Step 5: After you finish that first area –and only after you finish– move onto the next section of the room/space. It is so important to stay focused on one specific, manageable section at a time. Moving around is distracting and usually leads to time spent without much visible, tangible progress.

This is known as the "squirrel effect!"

HINTS FOR SMALL SPACES

- Not enough room for a nightstand or bedside table?

    Consider a floating shelf/shelves.

- Create a *DROP ZONE* near the edge of your dresser with a tray or dish for pocket clutter, hair ties, jewelry etc. to land until you store them in their regular places.

- Need book storage in a bedroom? Upcycle a small dresser: Remove the bottom two drawers to store books; the top drawer can hold extra bedside necessities.
- Hooks are ideal to hold items often dropped on the floor – pocketbooks, backpacks, umbrellas, etc.
- Pantry bulk items: empty boxed and bagged items into stackable containers. I recommend clear ones so you'll see at a glance what needs

restocking and the visual appeal is an additional, satisfying bonus for many. Don't underestimate the importance of labels!

CLOSETS For those of us who can't afford a closet redesigned to our needs with specialty units, try these ideas.

- Place baskets or bins on the floor to hold pocketbooks, shoes or to separate casual from dress shoes.

- Move the existing closet rod higher up and add a second lower rod to maximize space and organization.

- Utilize canvas closet organizers; an inexpensive solution to create storage zones. Six to eight compartments hanging vertically can separate sweaters, t-shirts, jeans, hats, scarves, and yes– even wigs.

- Place a shoe holder bag on the back of a closet door. All those many pockets provide neat, easy access to socks, underwear, leggings, slips, belts, clutches, hair accessories, sunglasses, etc.

"What would life be if we had no courage to attempt anything?'

-Vincent van Gogh

Chapter 2

Thinking Outside the Box

Moving to a new state was hard; we knew no one and most of my family was still in New Jersey. I had to figure out how to become my own person. In August of 1989, my new home in Hellertown, Pennsylvania was a place for me to really find out what I was made of and stretch my wings. I wasn't known as "one of the May kids" here; I was completely unknown, and this actually felt empowering. I was able to reinvent myself as a more self-assured individual, and I wanted to become part of this small town by serving it however possible.

Michael still worked in New Jersey, so I needed to learn the area, make connections and build relationships on my own. I did some volunteer work, but my greatest reward came from joining the Jaycees [Junior Chamber of Commerce], a civic organization for young business and community leaders. The Saucon Valley Chapter embraced me and guided me on the road to stepping out of my comfort zone. I went from being a member to holding various Board positions; I even served a one-year term as President.

Organizing events and keeping records definitely helped me on my present path. I learned the logistical processes required to get things done in an orderly manner –one step at a time– plus the importance of keeping accurate records so others could follow them. Those positions taught me confidence, leadership and patience while also teaching others.

Our finances were limited, so how did we make ends meet? We used coupons and bought reduced items at the grocery store. The girls wore some hand-me-down clothing from my nieces or the daughters of friends, and I shopped clearance racks or sale items. They often had the "in" styles only when they were about to become the "out" styles. Thankfully, either they never really noticed or just never complained about it. As older teenagers, both daughters babysat and held part time jobs to earn their own money and buy additional items they wanted if I was unable to do so.

During an extremely rough patch financially, Michael and I had no extra money for Christmas. Together, we made gifts for our girls that year. Michael was a talented woodworker, and I sewed a bit. Some things the girls had put on their Santa list were purchased for them by our wonderful families. They were young and never knew the difference. I also moderated what they requested by stipulating they could ask for no more than five items. They were also told Santa would do his best, but he might be able to bring only one of their requested presents.

I reused, upcycled and thought creatively when it came to storage, organizing, sorting, etc. Old lunch bags became first aid kits, empty diaper wipe containers became storage bins, shoe boxes and some of my Tupperware containers helped to organize drawers. The dollar stores and clearance sections were treasure mines to me. We used the local library for books, videos, and music CDs. One year Michael and I wanted to give the girls a backyard playhouse, but they were far too expensive. Walking through the local hardware store, we saw a small plywood shed. We bought it, Michael painted it, and I made curtains. Not only was it more affordable than an actual playhouse, it had our personal touch, and our girls were thrilled! We always made ends meet by putting our heads together, thinking outside the box and working as a team. We were pros at "making something out of nothing."

"I don't think outside of the box;

I think of what I can do with the box." -Destination Imagination

HELPFUL TIPS

Below are a few ideas on how to upcycle ordinary items into other uses. Thinking outside the box can be interesting.

Magazine holder

- store cleaning supplies under the sink –leave it freestanding or attach to the back of the door
- store cutting boards, baking sheets or cooling racks

- rolled washcloths and hand towels in a small bathroom – rolling them up keeps them neat and maximizes space

Shower Curtain Hardware

- attach eight rings on a strong hanger to hold sport caps
- attach multiple rings to a strong wooden hanger and loop scarves or ties through them

- place S-type hooks on a sturdy hanger to store belts by hooking the buckle on the lower curve

Wine Racks

- curling rod, flat iron, hairdryer (if vanity space permits)
- store water bottles in cabinet or pantry
- skeins of yarn, rolled or folded fabric remnants

Picture Frames

- Place game boards in frames with the playing pieces behind or inside the frame; hang them in the playroom (thanks to the unknown blogger who came up with this wonderful solution for damaged board game boxes)
- Paint glass with blackboard paint for a fancy, unique message board; use old-school chalk or chalk markers

- Hang smaller frames (with glass removed) around electrical outlets as decorative "covers"

Pencil Cases

- organize kids travel needs for sleepovers & camping trips
- fill with adult personal necessities such as toothbrush, toothpaste, dental floss, feminine products, razor, deodorant etc. to tuck into

briefcase or backpack in case

you get stranded at work or on

the commute

- portable first-aid kit

Coffee Filters

- lay between china/stoneware plates or frying pans
- insert in a mask as a filter
- make a tea bag for loose leaf

  tea; tie closed with string for a

full pot or use a thin popsicle

stick to suspend over a cup

Cookie Jars/Canisters (decorative)

- store cookie cutters
- hold pet treats
- store mesh veggie bags

Tension Rods

- Place a sturdy one under the

    kitchen sick and add open

curtain hooks to hang pots/pans or spray bottles
- No shelves in your shower? Place a tension rod on the back wall for washcloths, scrunch sponges & back brush
- Add a strong tension rod to a sunny window for hanging smaller potted succulents or plants

Shoe Caddy (ones with clear pockets are game changers!)

- in the pantry for snacks or oversized kitchen tools
- inside baby's closet for socks, bibs, rolled crib sheets, hats, mittens, smaller stuffed animals & toys
- on the back of a closet door for belts, ties, clutches, slips, stockings, jewelry

"Life is not about waiting for the storm to pass... It is about Learning to Dance in the rain."

-Vivian Greene

Chapter 3

Wow – NOT What I Planned!

Cancer threw fast, scary curveballs into my young family's life. 1994 started off as a good year, but by the end of April our lives were changed forever. I noticed one of Michael's socks was constantly bloodied. When he told me something must have fallen on his toe, which turned the nail black, I wasn't concerned. We figured it meant he was losing his toenail. The bloody socks stopped, but then his foot was stepped on during a game of basketball with my brothers and brothers-in-law, and the nail split in half. Now I love my husband, but the sad reality is he had a very high pain tolerance, and he refused to go to the podiatrist to have the nail removed, which drove me crazy. Finally, when the bloody sock returned daily and he was having difficulty walking, I gave him no choice. One July day when he arrived home from work I informed him we were leaving for the podiatrist office immediately, to have his toe examined. The doctor was amazing, told us straight away he didn't like what he saw, and he proceeded to take a biopsy. About two weeks later it was confirmed as cancerous.

Michael had melanoma carcinoma under his big toenail. We learned it was a rare spot to find cancer. By September 15 testing was complete, and his great toe was amputated. The surgeon shortened it enough so it was below the pressure point. Chemo or radiation were believed unnecessary as all lymph nodes up and down his leg to his groin area were clean. He was deemed fine. Whew, thank you Jesus!

As Thanksgiving approached, we were getting back to our "normal" lives– grateful Michael was feeling well and adjusting to the new balance on his left foot. In March 1995, he had his six-month check-up and all was still well.

Two weeks later, I found a lump in my left breast. I had been doing monthly self-exams for years, since my Aunt Nicki died from breast cancer and my Mom had fibrocystic breasts. A few weeks away from turning 35, I believed I was too young for breast cancer and expected I was probably fibrocystic like my mother. My doctor sent me for a mammogram, and while the lump did not show up on the x-ray, I felt it.

Always remember you know your body better than anyone else; if you feel something is wrong, don't give up looking for answers until you have exhausted every single avenue. My doctor agreed and scheduled an MRI, which unfortunately showed I was right– there was a lump! My relatively young age was exactly the reason it did not show up on the mammogram; my breast tissue was too dense. When my doctor/ surgeon aspirated the lump, the syringe contained a white, milky liquid— NOT A GOOD SIGN! I was alone when she told me I had a tumor, and the next step was a biopsy to determine if it was cancerous and if it had traveled to any lymph nodes.

My fear was confirmed when the lump was determined to be malignant. Since it was the high end of Stage 2, my choices were to undergo chemo treatments and leave the breast intact or have a mastectomy and then start chemo. The tumor was 5cm– which was the cutoff point for the decision to go either way. Michael and I discussed it, and he wanted me to decide which course of action to take. Since he had just gone through cancer, I wasn't taking any chances. We had two young daughters to raise! I felt the obvious choice was to go for the mastectomy and chemo so I could move forward with my life and we could all be healthy again.

On June 5, 1995 I had a lumpectomy, and the tumor was definitively malignant. On June 29, I had surgery and after the recuperation period my chemo treatments began. I must admit, losing my hair actually felt worse than losing my breast. I know vanity is unattractive, but my hair has always been the outward expression of my femininity.

With the help of my sisters Alaina and Colleen, and thanks to my father's generosity, we found a wig which allowed me to cover up when my hair began falling out. At first, our other siblings did not even notice I had started wearing a wig. Once chemo treatments were complete, I resolved to continue fighting and reassure our daughters I was strong and would fully regain my health.

We rang in 1996 feeling mostly okay. 1994-1995 absolutely sucked, quite honestly, but I was gaining my strength back and it had been a wonderful holiday season. Then cancer reared its ugly head once again. It was March 11, 1996, the night of our youngest daughter's birthday. Michael's melanoma returned with metastatic lesions on the upper lobe of his right lung. He underwent surgery to remove the upper lobe, then began self-administered Interferon shots. He said the way I jabbed the needle into a grapefruit for practice convinced him he should try injecting himself. I truly did not blame him. Our doctor set a one-year protocol for the Interferon. The strength it takes for a person to regularly stick themselves in the stomach for an entire year is simply amazing.

It feels important to state that we never, ever felt defeated or thought either of us was going to die. We made jokes about the body parts we were losing and how we might make up one whole person if this continued. You could visit us only as long as you were upbeat and positive; crying was not allowed. We stayed strong and determined. We had our little girls to live for so we fought hard!

Michael was feeling pretty good, and at each monthly checkup I was getting better. Our poor oncologist, Dr. Stephen Volk, was so upset by our cases and determined to help both of us beat the cancer beast. He often remarked, "You are such a young couple. I can't believe this is happening to you both at almost the same time."

In October 1996, fifteen months after my mastectomy, we decided it was time to either remove my extra breast tissue or do reconstruction. After discussions, I agreed to a tram-flap; my new left breast was constructed using stomach muscle they fished through my body. I told people, "Look, I received a tummy tuck, a new breast plus a breast reduction!" I was a new woman inside and out. An unexpected bonus to reconstruction surgery was it also removed the outer scar from the appendectomy I had at age 13.

While I was recovering from surgery, we learned Michael's cancer had now progressed into his liver and intestines. His medical team surgically removed the intestinal cancer, but the planned surgery on his liver was canceled because the liver had too many tumors, in too many places.

Now we were really in a fight for his life. They gave him two to four months, to which I said, "NO! He will live! We are a strong family and we will beat this." We sought further treatment ideas at Memorial Sloan Kettering. With a treatment protocol in place, we went back home where

Michael began receiving months of intense chemo, which was so hard on his body. We stayed at the hospital for one week each month so he could receive the treatment slowly, under sedation.

Every three weeks we had a regular office visit to learn if the tumors were shrinking. The results were no, then yes, then no, then yes... it was such a yo-yo on our emotions.

In October, 1997, after two consecutive months of encouraging results, Michael said he wanted to take our girls to Disney World. While I did not support the idea, I realized it was something he truly wanted and needed to do with them, and Dr. Volk approved a one-week delay for the next chemo session. Michael's mom gifted us the plane tickets, we stayed at her time-share, and she even joined us on the trip in case we needed help.

The girls were completely in the dark about our travel plans. Michael had arranged it to be a big surprise for them. Only the night before we left did they find out they would be taking their first flight, with Disney World as our destination. So off we went on our first family vacation, which would turn out to be our *only* full family vacation.

To say Michael was a new man once we landed in Florida is an understatement. He hadn't driven in months, walked very slowly and easily became out of breath. Yet none of that was true that week in Florida with his girls. I wanted him to use a wheelchair in the parks but he said no, and he was so full of energy he really did not need one. He was so vibrant and energetic, I started to believe we had finally crossed a bridge toward future test results being only positive news. Looking back, it was a magical week indeed.

Then we stepped off the plane in Pennsylvania, and he looked wiped out. His counts were a bit low, but they still allowed the full week stay for treatment. Unfortunately, November's results showed tumor growth, and in December they told us to wait for results until after the New Year.

On January 5, 1998 the doctors said nothing was working anymore and all treatments would stop, as his tumors were growing and spreading. Now he really might live only another two to four months longer. Since we had made that original time frame stretch to eight months already, I remained hopeful, but also began to prepare for the worst.

January 8, 1998: At 3:45 PM I called for an ambulance to take Michael to the hospital. He had collapsed for the second time that day as I was taking down our Christmas tree. After multiple tests and X-rays the ER doctors said he would not last the night. Just three days earlier we were told two to four months, so I didn't want to believe this dire new prognosis. My girlfriend called our eldest sisters; they in turn called all family members to alert them that whoever wanted to see Michael should come as quickly as possible.

He was moved to a room, and at 10:00 PM that evening we had our daughters brought to the hospital. I had to gently tell them their Dad was going to heaven. He had fought so hard but his body just couldn't take it anymore. Our daughters had no idea how sick their father was, since Michael and I had agreed we didn't want to scare or worry them unnecessarily. Obviously they knew we were both sick at times, but we did our best to carry on with as much normalcy as circumstances allowed. After learning all treatments would stop, we knew it was time to sit down with the girls and tell them.

In fact, we had the week fully planned out. Monday's bad news meant Michael needed a blood transfusion on Tuesday, and on Wednesday we would order a hospital bed. We would prepare a will on Thursday, spend Friday resting and digesting this new reality, and tell our daughters on Saturday. We got as far as Thursday morning when everything changed.

After we had our family time to say good-bye, the girls left with their aunt, and I stayed with Michael. I had my hand on his chest and felt his last heartbeat and watched his last breath. At 1:15 AM on January 9, 1998 he passed so peacefully from my arms into God's. I recount this story with so much detail so you might understand I do not give up easily. I am a strong, faith-filled woman who will never quit unless there is absolutely no other option.

As horrible as cancer is, it was also a bittersweet blessing.

Michael and I had been together since I was 16 and he was 18. He was –and still remains– the love of my life, my soulmate. We spent those last three years truly sharing everything we felt and needed to say. I never once left him in the hospital, and often slept on the floor until they finally gave me a chair.

3.5 years dating, married at 20, 17.5 years of marriage. Looking back, I know we genuinely lived our vows and we were each other's best friend. We lived a lifetime in those two-plus decades together. I feel incredibly blessed to have felt so loved and needed. We were true life partners.

"Accessibility is a necessity

that should never be

deprived."

-Robert M. Hensel

HELPFUL TIPS

Helping Those with Mobility Issues

- Accessibility is key. Does he or she live solo or is someone else there to help when needed?
- Place daily use items within easy reach –ideally between waist and chest height for best access.
- Consider the person's strength and ability to lift; how far can

she bend —if at all?

Infrequently used items can be placed on the higher or lower shelves.

- Cabinets with pull-out shelves are ideal if they exist in the home, or if it's possible to have them installed.

- Baskets and/or bins with handles or openings make them easier to grasp and pull forward.

- Place Lazy-Susans in corner cabinets. He or she can spin to retrieve items, and cabinet space is maximized.
- ALWAYS collaborate with the individual before you rearrange their space to ensure they feel 100% comfortable and secure with the changes.

A very personal upcycling story: It was an artificial tree I was undecorating when Michael passed away, so I made it "his tree." I took it apart, wove the branches together to form a cross and decorated it with ornaments and silk poinsettias: our family tree became a very special grave blanket. There have been 25 Christmas seasons since Michael's passing, and every single December I place it on his grave.

"Out of a mountain of despair, a stone of hope appears."

-Martin Luther King

Chapter 4

New Life

Michael's passing came with great sorrow, many challenges, burdens and decisions to be made. I am forever thankful for my family and friends who stepped forward to help me navigate through this horrible time.

Our finances were Michael's department and thanks to our combined medical expenses we were nearly broke. Only six days after he passed, I struggled to make the next mortgage payment. Two weeks later, my daughters and I received a most unexpected and absolutely amazing gift. The mortgage company returned the check with a letter stating I now owned our home free and clear. My beloved husband had taken out a special insurance policy when we bought the house almost nine years earlier. The plan he set in motion meant I would own the house outright if he predeceased me. This explained his comment to one of my girlfriends at the hospital that I would be better off if he died. I was so annoyed when I heard it. I assumed he said it because he felt he was becoming too much of a burden on us. My angel husband was watching over us. He gave us an incredible gift, the comfort and peace of mind to be able to stay in our safe and familiar home.

Being widowed and contemplating raising our daughters – then eight and 13– by myself was simply daunting. How was I going to earn enough money to support us, at a job that allowed me to be there for them, as well as continue our life as a family– no matter how differently things looked now. I kept the faith that everything would work out. I was determined to keep my deathbed promise to Michael; my number one goal was to keep our girls safe and well-cared for until they were each 21. It began with my job; I switched from nights to days, working the 9-2 shift so I could see the girls off to school and also be there before they returned home.

Bringing up my girls in a home where I no longer felt a single spot of serenity was filled with challenges. We had bought a fixer upper and weren't able to fix up much before we both got sick, and then he passed. This now became a job for "The Dunn Girls." I was equally determined to show my daughters we could do anything if we put our minds to it. Over the years, I repainted rooms, moved furniture around, and improved the landscaping.

There was one major change I needed to make after Michael passed; I needed to move out of our bedroom, which had always been my favorite space. It was extremely difficult for me to sleep there that I slept on the couch for months after his passing. Finally, I realized I needed to find my new serenity spot. I gave our room to elder daughter Dana and gave her carte blanche to make changes and decorate it however she pleased. She chose deep, sky blue walls with stenciled yellow stars and a ceiling full of glow-in-the-dark stars, arranged just like the constellations. Dana was – and still is– my celestial daughter.

Kelli, my youngest, was now free to decorate the room they had previously shared into a space all her own, and it has gone through multiple changes over the years. That room is now a haven for "snowflakes" as unique as my Kelli.

I moved from the couch to a sleeping bag in the uninsulated attic and planned to transform a small area into my serenity spot. I removed the door to allow the main floor heating to drift up the stairs and warm me.

It is so important to be able to step into your home and go to the place that gives you sanctuary from the world outside. Coming home and spending 15-20 minutes in your serenity spot can do wonders for your mental and physical health. When I do initial walk-throughs with my clients, I ask where their serenity spot is, and if it is truly the most peaceful, relaxing space. If it isn't, that is where we begin organizing and transforming.

Transitioning from wife and mother to widow and single parent made the years 1998-2001 some hard years indeed, but we stayed the course and did our best as a family of three. Deciding when and which of Michael's things to let go of was emotionally draining and called for deep soul-searching. Those decisions were important so we could continue to move forward. Michael is always with us in spirit, and we keep him alive in our favorite memories. That is his priceless legacy.

I wanted to prove to our girls we would be okay and that I was fine –despite having undergone cancer myself too– and set the intention to participate in the 24 Hour Relay For Life hosted by the American Cancer Society. I literally walked in a circle for 24 hours straight to help raise funds for ACS. I had Dana and Kelli walk by my side at the beginning, middle and mostly at the end of the walk, to help reinforce the "The Dunn Girls" mindset I would continue to instill in them; we three were a team. I continued walking the 24 hour Relay for Life for 10 more years. I had proven to the girls –and myself– I was strong and not going anywhere. At that point, I was 12 years cancer-free.

"If it doesn't add to your life, it doesn't belong in your life."

-unknown

Helpful Tips

Let it Go!

So often I hear clients say...

"They are gone now, so I have to keep that." They will ask... "Why can't I just let it go?" Sometimes they confess... "I don't know how to handle my feelings about this stuff." Letting go of a loved one's things is melancholy for some, and absolutely heart wrenching for others. I offer this advice based on ideas and solutions which have worked well for me and my clients; I hope it helps you too.

I believe there are three questions to ask once you feel ready to tackle this difficult task.

1. Do you want it?
2. Do you need it?
3. Will you use it?

4. Okay, there is a fourth question: Do you have an emotional attachment to it, and is it weighing on you?

I am convinced those no longer here on earth would not want us burdened with keeping their things out of guilt, if we don't need or want them. I'm sure the items were passed down to you with love, so you are not obligated to hold on to them indefinitely.

Suppose you were given a painting which isn't your style or doesn't go with your décor, you can choose to LET IT GO! and allow someone else to enjoy it. It's far better for your loved ones' items to be appreciated elsewhere, instead of remaining stored in a closet or under a bed.

Do you save old greeting cards? Unless they contain handwritten, personal messages which are special and meaningful to you, LET THEM GO!

What about a piece of clothing you've kept because you remembered someone wearing it, and they have now passed. Take a photo of the item, then LET IT GO! Donate it or give it to someone who will enjoy wearing it. You can also have it turned into a

pillow or a stuffed animal to hug.
Some clothing can be made into a
blanket, and you can literally wrap
yourself in the warmth of cherished
memories.

Remember YOU need to take a
breath, look at the item and either
take a photo to remember it or just
LET IT GO. Your peace and serenity are
paramount. We are not obliged to
hold onto "other peoples' stuff" until

WE die. We are here to enjoy this life and remember our loved ones with joy and happiness, free from the overwhelm of too many possessions and negative feelings. Declutter your emotions and your space once and for all.

"Challenges are what make life interesting and overcoming them is what makes life meaningful."

-Joshua J. Marine

Chapter 5

Finding a Career

Life threw me yet another challenge in 2001 when the grocery store I worked at was permanently closed. I needed a new job, but I didn't want *just* a job; I wanted a career.

Since my dream had always been to be a wife and mother, a career involving kids was my goal. I was a Girl Scout leader for years, and I had volunteered at both the elementary school and public libraries, helping with Circulation and Storytime. When Dana was in preschool, I was an Assistant Teacher at her school. Two months later, I was hired as Assistant Toddler Teacher at a school not quite 30 minutes away. I loved my new career, as it allowed me to get the girls off to school and arrive home not long after they did. With my nights free, I could still be a Girl Scout leader. I was thrilled to throw myself into my new career-job, which spoke to my passion and purpose. Let me tell you, I truly believe you are living your best life if you are doing something you find passion in.

I was paying for expensive COBRA insurance and while the school sought health insurance for me, they couldn't find a plan to cover only me, as the rest of the staff had insurance through their spouses. Since I had a pre-existing medical condition, I would become uninsurable unless I went from one plan directly to another, so I *had* to find a new school quickly. They understood and were so gracious about my leaving.

My angels were still watching over me, and I was hired at the

Community Center, a non-profit organization just down the street from my house. The Director actually contacted me first, to see if I would be willing to help teach at the center. She wanted to upgrade it from a daycare/babysitting service to a Child Care/Early Childhood Education school.

For the three and half years I worked at the Community Center I learned even more about organizing, upcycling, and using my creativity. At a non-profit it's imperative to have an outside-the-box mindset for sourcing materials and supplies economically, for storing them and stretching their usage.

My small classroom was home to a great many items. Utilizing the space well made the small room seem larger, and everything was easily accessible. In the hallway between my room and the preschool classroom I created a little library, which I carefully arranged to ensure full compliance with fire safety regulations.

"Upcycling turns things into other things which is basically magic."

-unknown

Helpful Tips

Classroom Ideas

Library Area

- Cut colored folders in halves, laminate them and label by genre, ensuring labels are visible at a glance
- Place magazines or special paperback books in clear page protector sheets; hang on a

tension rod with shower curtain clips

- Use extra large Ziploc bags with handles to stores books with tapes or CDs

Art Area

- Place crayons in dollar store baskets lined with colored construction paper cut to fit. Match the crayons to the liner colors. This helps with early learning matching skills.

- Transfer glitter into plastic salt and pepper shakers for easier use by small hands.
- Upcycled cookie sheets as art trays: each child uses one as a work space, which keeps desks neat, helps them carry supplies and makes cleanup faster/easier. It also works

great with magnets or magnetic items.

Inexpensive and/or Free Classroom Supplies

- Find low cost, donated or gently used items: at yard sales; dollar stores; book bag sales at libraries; from retired teachers, friends and family.

- Consider starting a classroom birthday tradition: the birthday child brings in a new book for the classroom library. Ask a parent of the birthday child to be the special reader that day for the book.
- Plastic tote bags from the dollar store or grocery store are perfect for travel size white boards, dry erase markers and a dry eraser. These are wonderful

for interactive writing times or drawing pictures during story time.

- Homemade musical instruments: upcycle pots, pans and lids, wooden or metal spoons, old-fashioned washboards, plastic containers partly filled with beans, bolts, marbles, or pebbles (be sure to glue the lids on tightly). Store the "instruments" in a bin to keep them neat and portable.

- Empty diaper wipe containers make good storage for small items. Dollar stores are a terrific resource for supplies needed for Math and Science areas. Taking your class on a Nature walk is a fun, educational and no-cost way to add to your Science materials.

"Just don't give up trying to do what you really want to do.

Where there is love and inspiration. I don't think you can go wrong."

-Ella Fitzgerald

Chapter 6

Being a Teacher

In May 2006, I left the Community Center for a teaching position at a brand new Child Care facility. Starting from scratch and working with corporate families was an exciting adventure. I called upon my organizing skills and imagination to shape a colorful, inviting classroom. Having theme-based lesson plans streamlined my work life, and I filled boxes with supplies I could use year after year. I arranged my space for both form and function and being frugal was still important.

When you share resources – whether art supplies, toys, or items for the various educational areas in different classrooms– things must be organized for easy access and proper returns. Since I welcome a challenge, when I volunteered to help to keep the art supply room and storage racks holding classroom supplies neat and tidy, I reorganized both areas so we could then maintain them effortlessly.

Teachers cannot help but think "outside the box" and creatively as funding is not always available for new items. Most teachers spend their own money to keep classrooms fresh and exciting for their students. Being a savvy upcycler and DIY-er is almost a necessity for any teacher. Showing kids how all of us can help the environment by reusing or repurposing items is also socially conscious, mentally stimulating and can be fun!

"Your kids are wildflowers,

Give them space to grow."

-Maxine Lagac`e

Helpful Tips

Updating Your Child's Room

How many times have you heard, "I want a big kid's room!" It's entirely possible to make it an easy, inexpensive upgrade. First, rethink the floor plan. Move the bed into another position, then the dresser, desk and other furniture in the room. Relocate most toys to the playroom, choosing only a few special items to stay in the bedroom.

Remove wallpaper borders or wall decals which have "kiddie" motifs. Paint the walls and trim if they need a refresh or if your child longs for a different color. Hang posters in inexpensive frames or maybe you have a budding artist who wants to personalize the room with his or her own creations.

Updating the bedding and window coverings creates an instant upgrade. If they still want to have a themed room, consider a solid color for curtains and comforter/bedspread, and bring the theme in with the sheets and throw pillows.

Remember, when updating a room, it is an ideal time to LET GO of items no longer being used. There is no need to keep kiddie themed bedding, accessories, toys etc. unless they can be used to update a younger child's room. If not, and if they are in serviceable condition, donate them.

"The expert in anything

was once a beginner."

-Helen Hayes

Chapter 7

Fixer-Upper

As I noted earlier, the house Michael and I bought was a true fixer-upper. My education in home improvement was not easy, but again my determination kicked in. The father of one of my students worked construction and for just the cost of materials, he generously built me a front porch. I was grateful for kind neighbors and friends who took time to teach me home maintenance tasks and small repairs. When any type of work was being done at my home, I made sure I was there so I could learn the process. I sincerely appreciate the helping hands of those willing to teach me.

When my oldest daughter Dana left for college, I wanted to surprise her with a new look to the house when she returned for Thanksgiving break. The living room paneling needed to go, and I was fortunate to have a friend willing to help me remove it and begin the tedious process of spackling the walls. I wasn't the best at it but we got the job done, and I still use those spackling skills whenever I update paint colors. Next,

I wanted to remove the hallway wallpaper and paint both areas. Let me just state for the record, I hate painting! However, painting is usually the easiest and most affordable way to refresh the look and feel of a space. I have repainted my living room and hallway three times and the bedrooms a couple of times too.

I've given my kitchen a much needed facelift several times over the years simply by painting the cabinets. These kinds of updates inevitably lead to decluttering and inviting in newfound serenity. During those times I consciously worked on letting go of Michael's items.

Grieving isn't a once and done process. With each milestone my daughters marked, I needed to make one too.

Over the years I evolved into a new and improved person. I would always be Michael's wife, Carmela's and Charlie's daughter, the baby sister/older sister to my five siblings, but now I was in growth mode, and continuously learning and enhancing my strengths—physically, emotionally and spiritually.

Listening to my inner voice brought me happiness. I was always open to learning new repurposing and upcycling tricks to stretch both my budget and my creativity. Now I was learning how my life's struggles and challenges actually gave me skills which led to gratifying volunteer roles: supporting cancer patients working through the process; offering a soft shoulder and understanding ear to recent widows/widowers; and helping newly single parents adjust to so many unknowns. I knew helping others was important and also therapeutic for me, but I also found it incredibly uplifting.

"You can do anything you

set your mind to."

-Eminem

Helpful Tips

INSTALLING A NEW DOOR LOCK (and other home tasks)

- The easiest way I found to change a lock is to buy the same brand of lock. Remove the original lock piece by piece. [Taking photos or a video will be key –HAH! – to follow the correct order when putting it back together.] Redrill holes if needed. Stay calm, focused and believe you can do it!

- Plant flowers and shrubs to update your outdoor spaces. Choose your favorite perennials and enjoy the return on your investment year after year. Add seasonal annuals in spring and autumn if your time and budget permit.
- Changing cabinet hardware for a new look in the kitchen is

another way to give a quick facelift.

- If you are a good painter or enjoy the process, painting furniture is an inexpensive update.
- Installing blinds: Measure inside window frame, choose your style/color and place order. Mark holes for brackets; use a manual or electric screwdriver to put the screws in, then

unscrew them. As you put brackets in place, drill the screws back in securely. Hang those blinds with confidence and enjoy the results of your labor!

Getting Kids Ready for Dorm Life

Investing time and patience to teach kids organizational skills at a young age will pay them dividends their entire lives. I have seen firsthand how a college student living in a small, well-organized dorm room can function with calm and focus –or the exact opposite –a student who feels anxious and stressed while trying to live and study in a messy, disorganized space. Teach kids to evaluate needs vs. wants, how to use things in multiple ways, and the benefits of practical items like

Command strips and surge protector/power strips.

"Collect moments not things."

- **Karen Salmansohn**

Chapter 8

Letting Go

I sorted and organized many of my Mom's things in early 1989 before we moved out. But when Dad passed away in 2007, we had to purge our family home on a grand scale so it could be staged and sold. Wow—the emotional roller coaster ride you take while sifting through and holding tangible items which revive childhood memories– it is powerful. I did basic decluttering and then arranged items so my siblings could help make choices. There were some tough choices. Deciding what we wanted to keep because of the attached memories and what should be donated brought in a new chapter of grieving. My eldest sister Alaina took the reins handling all charitable donations. My brothers Chuck, Andrew and Curtis handled the grounds and the garage with help from our brothers-in-law Fred and Len. My sister Colleen proved excellent at evaluating which items each of our respective children might like to have to remember their grandparents.

The entire process was overwhelming and mentally draining,

yet most of the time I also found joy in the treasures. I found, and I grew excited while hunting for important papers. It actually ignited my desire to organize more. I realized the consequences of leaving this job for others to handle, especially the newly bereaved. Each of us should make time to examine our things and begin the process of letting go. If you wish certain items to go to specific people when you pass, make it a priority to compile and keep it with your will and other important papers– all of which should be in good order.

Organizing became my new passion, and by 2015 I was helping friends and family declutter and organize their spaces.
I started a list of charitable organizations and outreach programs which offered donation pickups or had drop off locations. I focused on

well-run operations seeking good quality items to help those in need.

After two years of helping others sporadically, I started to think about retiring from teaching. I instinctively felt a grand, new adventure awaited me. But I needed to pace myself and make it my first priority to figure out the bottom line financial and health insurance aspects to pull off a career change.

"If your stuff isn't serving you, it won't be serving you any better packed away in a box somewhere."

-Melissa Camara Wilkins

Helpful Tips

MOVING

When you make the big decision to move, it's never too soon to begin packing. That's right –begin purging and packing as soon as you know a move will be happening. Gather these critical supplies before you start:

1. Sturdy boxes
2. Bubble wrap / paper to protect breakables
3. Permanent markers

4. Packing tape

5. Bins for the items to be stored

6. Floor plan or layout of your new home

Start with those rooms, areas and items you will not use during the moving process. Next pack the items you will use least and save daily necessities for absolute last. As you pack, be sure you really love, need and want the items. This is the best time to purge, because clutter is the last thing you want in your new place. Also, if you need to hire a moving company, you won't be paying to have things transported only to discard them at the new place. Remember— start packing early for an efficient and cost effective transition!

Label boxes and bins by category or by contents. Mark boxes to clearly designate which room/space each box should be placed in the new home. This is where a floor plan or at least the names of the rooms is helpful. If you do not have a floor plan, here is an example: The bathroom is on the first floor so label the box 1BA; the kitchen is also on the first floor, so label kitchen items 1K. If you do have a floor plan: number each room on the plan and place that number on the box. I recommend a thick marker in a bold color to number the boxes. Use a thick red marker to write FRAGILE on those boxes requiring delicate handling.

Next, make a list of places to donate unwanted items and note which ones offer to pick-up. Now, evaluate items outside your home as well:

- Will you take any or all lawn and garden accessories?

    (planters, birdhouses, wind chimes etc.)

- Outdoor furniture and yard work tools?

- Do all items have places at the new home or is it best to donate or leave behind for the new owners?
- Are there any plants or small trees which have meaning to you? If you decide to take them, be sure to replace them–or at least fill in any empty holes.

When you declutter, be mindful you don't make decisions for your spouse or partner. You can downsize and organize while still being respectful of their items. Avoid potential rifts and resentment from wrongly assuming they don't need or want a certain thing, which in reality may be quite important to them. I recommend placing their items in an area for them to evaluate and make their own decisions. Collaboration will make for a smooth transition to your new home and serenity for one and all.

"Let Your FAITH be bigger than your fear."

-1700 Theologian John Wesley

Chapter 9

New Life Path

On New Year's Eve of 2016 I resolved to change the way I ate, determined to lose extra weight. I would turn 57 in April, and I felt unhappy with my body and my life. So on January 1, 2017 I started a 30-day Paleo challenge during which I avoided all gluten, dairy, sugar, salt and processed food. Only the most healthy, natural foods and beverages would go in my body. I put smaller portions on my plate, ate meals more frequently and drank 128 ounces of water per day. Sadly, this also meant no more wine.

As the weight dropped off, I felt energized and proud of myself. I was becoming more creative with food preparation, which fed my creativity in other ways. This was–and still is–a lifestyle change and not a diet. My mindset was becoming healthier and I was moving toward my sixth decade with a more clearly defined purpose.

After four diligent months of my new eating plan and lifestyle, I made it a priority to purge my closets of all clothing which was now too big and all cookbooks I no longer used. I donated my old plateware which had oversized plates and replaced it with a new set of dishes with modest proportions.

I was more convinced than ever I was ready to retire from teaching and open my own business as a professional organizer. Teaching just wasn't bringing me the joy and satisfaction it used to, and it was time to regain serenity in my work life.

I took a vacation week in June 2017 and thought, "If I find insurance during this week off, I will retire from teaching for good." I prayed hard and the good Lord answered my prayers; by Tuesday I had found insurance! Next, I took an extreme leap of faith. When I returned to school Monday morning, after 15-plus years at my teaching job, I tendered my resignation and gave a one-month notice. It would take me a month to remove all my things from my classroom and take them home.

My last day as a teacher was July 21, 2017. I genuinely love "my kids" and their parents, who threw me a wonderful retirement party and were so generous with their good wishes and gifts. I was able to buy a laptop for my business and much needed supplies. They also presented me with a binder full of memories and messages from my present and past students and families. I felt so blessed then, and I still feel the blessings of those relationships. I am thankful many of the families and I remain connected to this day.

A funny thing about starting a business is, you really should know – before you begin– that all your ducks are in a row legally and financially, and you can pull this thing off. I can laugh about it now, but I knew nothing. Thank God a wonderful Attorney in town shared his wisdom for free with me. Just because you want something doesn't mean it will happen overnight. Not knowing all the legalities and requirements can shut you down or result in fines. Again, I thank God I was able to get my business housekeeping in order quickly. Taking this leap of faith really brought me closer to my actual Faith.

God has never let me down. He does keep me waiting at times, and that's when I use my creativity to promote my business and attract paying clients.

With the full support of Dana, Kelli and my son-in-law Ben, I started "Donna's A Place For Everything." I give full credit and gratitude to my brother-in-law Len for naming my business. While we were all together for a family occasion, I had everyone cast votes for the name they liked best and Lenny's suggestion won. My girls said they were so happy I was doing something for myself after all I had done for them. Their vote of confidence was a big morale booster for me!

I was very busy the first month of my retirement. I learned to build a website and create a Facebook

Business page; I designed and ordered business cards and letterhead. I was also spending time reorganizing my home since I had brought back so much from my classroom. Realizing before-and-after photos would be a critical marketing tool, I compiled a gallery to show potential clients how my abilities could transform their spaces for the better.

I might as well confess, I am horrible with technology. My poor daughters can go over the same information time and again, and while I listen intently and really do try to grasp the information, it never seems to gel to the extent I can do it on my own. Dana is the family computer whiz; from her home a four-hour drive away, she created a slideshow for the website.

My daughter Kelli lives with me and is my #1 cheerleader —and the person who talks me off the edge when the inevitable computer issues arise. Thankfully, she too is tech-savvy and can fix almost anything I mess up. Ahh, the blessing of technology and the people who can master it!

With any startup business it's crucial to reach as many potential customers as possible, within your budget and available time. I planned Inspirational Quotes to post on Social Media on Tuesdays, and going into the weekend I offered Frustrated Friday Tips. Social Media was the quickest way I could build a following without spending a dime.

In late August 2017, an extended family member hired me to help organize three different spaces in her home. I was overjoyed and anxious to work again. Sandi, I'm so grateful to you for being my first official client; I appreciate you entrusting me to help you find the peace and serenity you longed for in your home.

When helping clients, my philosophy is to listen to their issues and wishes and create an action plan. We then begin in one corner of the room or space and work around it, hand in hand, together. When I started I went to homes with three bins and a box of trash bags. One bin was for donations, one for sellable items and one for things that belonged in another room. It is important to stay focused on one space at a time; and the last 30 minutes of our session is reserved to move items to their proper place in other rooms. I find most clients have many things already in their homes which are useful to separate and organize. It's not always necessary to spend money on organizing tools.

To help my clients move through those emotionally taxing decisions, I ask many questions: What meaning does this hold for you? Do you like it, use it, is it in good condition, does it go with your current decor, does it fit you, do you feel good wearing it? I listen with understanding and empathy because items often have stories, and as they share the history of a thing or their relationship to the person who gave it to them, their stress is real and visible as they decide what to keep and what to release.

I feel it's important to share my own stories with clients since they are being so open and vulnerable with me. I'm always mindful of how personal the "letting go" process can be. They need and want my help, but often are overwhelmed and anxious even about getting started. I reassure them they and their things are in safe hands, and I believe my sharing does make them more comfortable. Each individual also approaches the process with their own beliefs and thoughts about their stuff. Ultimately, I respect their feelings and wishes, even if I gently disagree and challenge them a bit.

Example: A client inherited everything from her parents, who kept literally EVERYTHING. She didn't want to disrespect their memories by throwing things out or even giving them away. She felt obligated to keep it all. Unfortunately, this meant her place was jam packed with unwanted items, negative energy and a bit of anger too. I asked if she thought her parents would want her living this way –with negativity and resentment– or did they leave everything to her out of love? We both knew the answer. When she stated out loud that of course they would want her to be happy and have only good feelings about their material bequest, then it became much easier for her to part with things. There was so much she didn't need, didn't have any sentimental attachment to or didn't even like.

I shared my history of holding on to items that were my parents' and my husband's for quite a while after they had passed and how I came to realize I was living with the negative energy of these unwanted, unused things. They were taking up too much space in my small home and felt suffocating. Once I released them, I felt so much lighter and relaxed in my space. Of course I held on to certain items, but only because I really wanted them. My client cried at some points –and she has not been the only one to do so– going through the additional mourning process of letting things go. This is healthy, necessary and can be life changing. At the end of the day she was smiling, feeling lighter and brighter. She was well on the path to finding serenity in her space.

When an area has been transformed and I look into a client's eyes, I see satisfaction, sometimes relief, and a more relaxed, peaceful person. I have done my job and helped make a difference in their lives. I chose my helping hands logo for this reason. The lower hand (client) reaches up for a hand to help guide them, and the upper hand (me) reaches down to lead them out of the chaos and into serenity.

"If you need motivation to LIGHTEN your life, think how your donations will ENLIGHTEN others."

-Donna L Dunn

Helpful Tips

Life Changing Events

When we experience life changing events like illness, death, job loss or our body changing, these challenging and emotionally dark times can actually lead us to bright new beginnings. After significant –or even minor weight loss you can let go of clothing which now hangs on your body. I recommend keeping only a few items from your previous size; more than a few could lead to a defeatist mindset: "Well, if I gain the weight back at least I'll still have a full wardrobe." NO! You released those pounds and inches; now release the emotional weight of pessimism and negative energy. Embrace your new look; you are living your best life from this moment forward. I suggest a three to six month timeframe maintaining your lower weight before fully purging your closet and making extensive clothing purchases. Box up a few of your favorite old, larger items and store them away. After six months or so, donate them to a worthy cause such as Turning Point, a safe haven for battered and abused women. Consider donating to organizations which help struggling women (or men) get back on their feet and dress appropriately for job interviews. Homeless shelters are always grateful for donations of clothing, shoes and accessories to distribute to the needy. A natural disaster in your area (fires, floods and hurricanes, etc.), presents an opportunity for your unneeded items to immediately help people who are displaced and suffering.

Once you are healthy and thriving after a major life change, you can support others experiencing challenges. I love to encourage my clients to shift their thinking away from the monetary value of items they are giving up and instead focus on the warm, uplifting feelings they will gain from bringing ease and comfort to people in need. I tell them "Let's lighten your life by enlightening others."

Cookbooks

If you are eating differently now such as Paleo, Keto, gluten free, etc., many of your old cookbooks may no longer serve you. Donate them to libraries, schools, senior centers and even Girl Scout or Boy Scout troops.

Lighten your bookshelves like you have lightened your body!

Kitchen Appliances

Evaluate your small appliances and honestly assess if you use them enough or they primarily take up cabinet space. If you no longer eat fried food, let go of the deep fryer. If a regular toaster will suffice, donate that big toaster oven. If you're downsizing and certain things won't fit in the new home or if you no longer cook for a large family …let them go! Replacing them with more streamlined –and possibly multi-functional– appliances which can do even more than all the old ones combined.

"You are never too old to set another goal or to dream a new dream."

-C.S. Lewis

Chapter 10

Starting a Business

Assembling as much information about your state and local government rules for running a business should be the first thing you do as an entrepreneur. Make sure all your proverbial ducks are in a row and you are in full compliance. Purchase all the necessary business insurance even before you land that first client. Open checking and saving accounts in your business name. You may want to hire an accountant from the start to help you keep accurate records. That said, I didn't have an accountant until it was time to tackle my 2017 tax return. I am happily, hopelessly old-fashioned so I was keeping my own books with paper and pencil. As I kept my records month by month, I was reminded of my Mom and her household bookkeeping, and it made me feel closer to her.

In the early part of my entrepreneurial journey, I invested time learning about Facebook for Business, Instagram, Marketing and Networking to promote my business. Fortunately, the internet has an endless supply of sites, blogs and podcasts where many successful professionals offer up their knowledge and expertise. One of my favorites is Carrie Green and her Female Entrepreneur Association (FEA), and she has inspired me tremendously. I knew how I wanted my business to work, but I did not know the best ways to promote it. I learned quickly by taking online courses and watching webinars daily. Again, I owe endless thank yous to my daughters Dana and Kelli for their patient explanations and willingness to demonstrate when I struggled to comprehend. I practiced taking photos to teach myself how to get the best angles and capture impactful shots which told a transformation story. Taking the "after" photo from the same exact spot as the "before" is something I'm still trying to master. But I remind myself I am a work in progress– aren't' we all?

"Your Home is a Living Space, not a Storage Space."

-Francine Jay

Helpful Tips

Things We Gloss Over

Let's talk about a few items we tend to not see as clutter.

- Glass vases from floral deliveries: How many do you really need to keep? Evaluate their sizes, shapes and colors to help you choose.
- Place settings: Do you have cracked or chipped cups, plates,

bowls, glasses and maybe some flatware pieces that took a spin in the garbage disposal? If you tell yourself they're still functional and yet you worry about being cut, further breakage or who might use that damaged piece, then it's time to let them go. If you are an artsy-craftsy type, you may see creative possibilities instead of trash. You can also donate them to a recycling/upcycling shop. I have a local place called Tinker'N LV which finds uses for discarded items. You can show the environment some love while helping others exercise their creativity on the cheap.

- Bed linens/sheet sets: Examine and evaluate their condition. If they are sized for beds or mattress sizes you no longer have, let them go. How many sets do you need for each bed? Two is my number, but I do keep extra pillow cases in case of head colds, nosebleeds etc.

- Garage/shed items: camping gear, outdoor games and sports equipment no longer being used by anyone in the home? Let them go to others who will appreciate them.
- Bathroom tools: Hairbrushes, curlers, straighteners, hair care

products and the like just taking up the often limited vanity storage space, time to let them go!

When is the Best Time?

When should you reduce the items in your closet? First, if you're asking this question, then the time is NOW!

Second, if you become anxious, stressed, or simply uncomfortable whenever you go into a certain closet, dresser, or room, that's the perfect time to assess the contents and ask yourself the important questions.

1. Do I need it?
2. Do I like it?
3. Have I used it or worn it in the last six months?
4. How does it make me feel?
5. Is it just taking up space?
6. Lastly, the all-important question, WHY do I still keep it?

Whether visible or stored out of sight, if something feels heavy and burdensome it is not good for you. So just let it go!

"All our dreams can come true if we have the courage to pursue them."

-Walt Disney

Chapter 11

Coming Out of My Shell

Over the past few years I have definitely come out of my shell and emerged as a businesswoman. I have done group presentations through a hospital and for networking groups, many of them in person and due to Covid-19, even more of them virtually.

This stage in my life has been filled with rapid changes and exciting challenges. I purchased equipment and began recording short videos. Remember, technology is not my forte but my stubborn persistence has paid off. It hasn't all gone as planned, but I have also had many "WOW" moments. Doing my "Inspirational Quotes" reaffirms why I chose to open my business. Writing my "Frustrated Friday Tips" has been a weekly adventure to share what I know, what I have learned, and what I have personally used. I love teaching others to think outside the box and expand their creativity. Magic often happens when my clients and I bounce ideas off each other. They are confident they can maintain the newly organized space. I am happy and proud of their efforts toward finding their own personal serenity.

I like to challenge clients –and myself– to seek out things already in their home to help organize their spaces. We can get the job done well without having to spend much money. My mission is to help people find Peace and Serenity in their space so they can live lighter and less stressed lives. Removing the literal and figurative heaviness of excess stuff, negative energy, and invoking only positive vibes with streamlined, organized spaces can raise the vibration, increase positive energy and lead to happier people.

"It's not about what it is-

It's about what it can

become!"

-Dr. Seuss

Helpful Tips

Upcycling Baskets

Most of us have varied sizes of baskets which we received filled with gifts or purchased ourselves. They often become dust collectors, rarely if ever used. Perhaps we pull them out a few times a year to arrange food for occasions or holidays, etc. Let's explore other ways to put them to work.

BATHROOM

- Place a medium to large sized basket on the floor when there is no linen closet. Roll up washcloths, several hand towels and two bath towels.
- A basket on top of the tank for extra rolls of toilet tissue.
- No medicine cabinet? Let a rectangular

basket neatly hold frequently used skincare and makeup items.

LIVING ROOM/FAMILY ROOM

- Small: Keep remotes neat and accessible

- Place just a few magazines you intend to read in a basket; don't overload it or it will become a clutter spot.

- Medium sized: Contain mail as it comes into the house– a drop zone until you're ready to open it.
- Small to medium: Arrange a few childrens' books with either seasonal or holiday themes.

- Medium size: Nestle a few toys and stuffies for the grandkids (or other littles) to enjoy while visiting.
- Medium to large: Corral pet toys and balls so they're not scattered all over the house and pets can easily grab them (major kudos if you can teach them to put them

back IN the basket when they're done playing).

- Small size: to hold coasters
-

FOYER/ENTRYWAY

- A basket on a small table or shelf to drop driving gloves, keys, sunglasses, masks, maybe a mini bottle of hand sanitizer. If space doesn't permit, find a home for these items in the kitchen.

KITCHEN

- Use a 9" x 13" sized basket for the kids' daily school papers you need to review each day.
- Aromatic like onions, garlic and shallots will be happier until you're ready to use them if

stored in a basket which allows them to breathe

SEWING ITEMS

If you have a small space to serve as a sewing area, make the most of that space with the tips below. Use the vertical space for shelves, thread holders, peg boards, magnetic strips, etc. Think outside the box, of course!

- hang shoe holders with clear pockets over the

door for tape measures, chalk, pincushion, etc.

- multi-rung pant/skirt hangers to neatly store fabric

- peg boards to hang ribbons and thread spools

- filing cabinet to store fabrics and trims; organize them by colors, textures, patterns and styles

- hang one or more magnetic strips for scissors, covered metal tins or jars with metal tops. Use them to store pins, beading, buttons, needles, snaps, etc.
- food storage bins can hold zippers, fabric scraps, patches, iron-on transfers, decals

- hang wire magazine racks on the wall to store and easily access patterns and project magazines
- convert a desk into a sewing table: a center drawer can hold rulers, cutting items, fabric tools, pens and markers. Use small containers to keep the other drawers neat and organized. If

there's a file drawer, store patterns and fabrics there. Place an ironing mat or a cutting mat on top of the desk.

- If there is a couch or bed in the new sewing room, utilize the space underneath for storage—long plastic storage bins are an ideal choice.

UPCYCLING: LUNCH BAGS

How to repurpose lunch bags the children loved getting at the start of each new school year? If they're in good condition, here are a few ideas:

- Hold art supplies for children to bring to restaurants and stay busy while you have adult conversation

- First-aid kit for car, truck, boat or home

- Sewing kit for a young beginner or hooks and yarns for first time knitters/crocheters

- Carrying case for small cars, trucks or figurines

- Card games for camping trips, picnics or the beach

- Toy medical bag for kids (the plastic containers they come in usually break soon after being opened)

- Storage/carrying case for Legos, Duplos, Shopkins, etc. or doll clothes and accessories

"Difficult roads lead to beautiful destinations."

-Zig Ziglar

Chapter 12

Networking

Having participated in several business networking groups, I am sure Karen Joseph's Arizona-based SEVEN Networking group is the very best. Karen relocated to the Southwest from New York and founded her business with the certainty there was a need for a group which focused more on developing personal relationships and connections among entrepreneurs, versus being overly concerned with referrals.

In April 2019, I joined the Catasauqua, Pennsylvania chapter. SEVEN stands for Supporting and Empowering the Vision of Entrepreneurial Networking. I learned to make 30-60 second commercials in a Marketing class, but in SEVEN Networking meetings Karen calls such commercials "magical networking moments." Members present a commercial at every meeting, which builds confidence in public speaking and the ability to "sell" your business without being pushy. It helped me to more clearly define what I do with and for my clients, to understand the true mission of my business, and to evolve the business into a more well-rounded company.

I was glad to join the local SEVEN Networking Chapter because the members were so warm and inviting. I had been struggling to get my business known beyond word of mouth and the monthly leads from a national business directory, which cost more than the income those leads generated during the two years I subscribed. I canceled it and researched other options. I did one more massive mailing introducing myself and my business to senior centers, assisted living facilities, Realtors, and senior living developments. One local Realtor was kind enough to invite me to her networking group. I can't thank Janice enough for opening my life to this wonderful community of ladies and the country-wide SEVEN Networking group.

Sharing information about your business can be thrilling and uplifting. Each week I told the group about my passion and explained why/how it became my passion, which continuously grew my confidence that I would become successful. The women cheered me on and offered great suggestions for growing my business too. There is never a competitive or selfish aspect at these meetings. We encourage and support one other, true to founder Karen's relationship model for SEVEN Networking.

Karen has been a welcome beacon for me and so many others looking to make and grow real connections. My passion is to help people, and the personal nature of my business makes it necessary for me to get to know people if I'm to bring their organizing goals to reality. I'm happy to say many clients become friends by the time we finish their projects.

Around this time Covid-19 hit, and life as we knew it changed dramatically. For many months we were on lockdown and were forced to radically alter how we ran our businesses just to keep them going, as well as maintain our networking connections. Thankfully the online meeting platform Zoom provided a safe, viable way for local and national groups to connect. And connect I did— I was able to meet groups all over the USA and around the world, while still building close personal relationships. Zoom became my close friend!

The feedback and encouragement I have received from members of so many different SEVEN Networking chapters is priceless. Their input and support helped increase my confidence every day as I talked about Donna's A Place For Everything during multiple Zoom meetings. I was able to make new friends and support other small businesses all over.

While the pandemic may have kept us home, it also encouraged us to think outside the box on a grand scale. We had to learn to pivot and not only keep our businesses afloat, but to thrive personally. When you share your passion and knowledge to help others, life can surprise and delight you with some very good moments even in very bad times.

Speaking of surprises, if anyone had told me I would write a book someday, I would have said "No way!" —and that it wasn't even a desire for me. I can't help laughing at that thought as I sit here now writing it. Covid-19 was my springboard to intense growth: conquering technology to make those videos and do Facebook Live sessions to get Donna's A Place For Everything in the public eye; virtually networking across the country and even globally; contributing a chapter to a collaborative book; and writing my own book. I am proud of how far I've come in a few short years.

When Susan (Suki) Jeffreys interviewed me for her Courage Rises program, she asked where I thought my courage and strength came from, was I always this way or did life experiences forge those characteristics? The answer is twofold. I told Suki I grew strong and courageous because I had no choice but to survive! I needed to raise my girls on my own, to reassure them their mother was well and we would carry on as a family, despite the changed dynamic when they lost their Dad and I lost my other half. Cancer took their Dad, but I had beat mine and was getting stronger and stronger.

A second and likely deeper reason for my strength is that it's a legacy from my mother. My Mom always exuded a calm, confident presence in any room. Not to say my Dad wasn't a strong person, but Mom inherited her palpable strength from her own incredible mother, who emigrated from Sicily as a young woman and nearly died on the difficult, three-week ocean crossing spent in the dark, dirty, overcrowded steerage of the ship. I'm proud to come from a long line of strong Sicilian women. Okay, sometimes strong crosses over to stubbornness.

Suki then asked how I was becoming braver or finding even more courage. I responded that I needed to get out of my own way and out of my head. Overthinking sometimes caused me "analysis paralysis" and stopped me from following through on ideas. I had often let fears get the better of me and I wanted to put a stop to that. I believe you can do anything if you put in the effort, educate yourself and ask for help when necessary.

"Having a simplified uncluttered home is a form of self-care."

-Emma Scheib

Helpful Tips

Home Office

FILING SYSTEM

- Use hanging divider folders with tabs to create categories and regular folders within those. You may prefer sticking with basic manila or primary colors, but file folders are available now in a dizzying array of colors and designs.

- To better see tabs, keep them all to the right or left side.
- Empty the file cabinet at the beginning of each year. If you are not sure what needs to be saved, consult with your accountant and/or attorney.

DESK TOP

I can almost guarantee if you work this simple system your desk will stay neat and you'll avoid paperwork overwhelm:

1. IN
2. OUT
3. ACTION

INBOX – Unopened mail and items to be handled or delegated

OUTBOX – Items to be filed and outgoing mail

ACTION BOX – Active projects (planning, to do lists, bills to be paid, forms to be completed, notes or cards to write)

SHREDDING

Shred all papers containing sensitive information such as your signature, account numbers, Social Security number, date of birth, driving license number, medical information and financial or legal information. When in doubt check out this website for a complete list:

www.fightidentititytheft.gov

FIVE FREQUENTLY ASKED QUESTIONS

1. Are you responsible for keeping your adult childres's items?
    a. No! My rule is, if you move out SO DO YOUR THINGS. Any items you leave behind will be handled at the discretion of the parents. When grown kids

strike out on their own, parents must not feel guilty about reclaiming spaces in their home to do with as the please. Remember it is the parents' home not a storage shed.

2. Do we need to keep knickknacks just because someone we know gave them to us?

a. NO! Keep only what brings you joy and happiness, and nothing that weighs you down or feels stressful when you see it.

3. Should I upcycle items instead of tossing them?

   a. YES! Google "DIY, upcycle, repurpose" for endless ideas.

4. Should I declutter before a move?

a. YES! This ensures you will pack only those items you really want, need and will use at your new home.

5. When is the best time to sort holiday decorations?

   a. I think there are three good times:

- As you are placing decorations and trimming the tree, if you don't use them all, ask yourself why and maybe the answer is to let them go?

- As you store items away, check their condition. Consider if you will even want to have the same look next year.

- Pleasant spring/summer weather makes for a good time to pull out decorations and examine them and allows you to make unhurried decisions versus during the busier holiday seasons. If you choose to make changes or replace items, it is easier with that knowledge from the start of the holiday season. The selections are better; you are not rushed and have time to look.

DECORATIVE BOXES & BOOKS

Decorative books and boxes are great for organizing.

- Place prayer/memory cards from deceased loved ones and set the "book" on a shelf. No one else knows what is in it, but they are within easy reach for you.
- Fill with correspondence items including pens, stamps, return address labels, envelopes, stationery or specialty cards. It can even double as a lap desk.

Just open your "book" and sit down to write!

- No desk? Use for office supplies like business cards, pens, receipt pads, gift cards, etc. Place on a shelf near whatever space serves as a makeshift home office.
- Let children choose boxes to store homework/class project materials at the table or counter. Everything

they need is in one place for

easy access and cleanup.

"The biggest adventure you can take is to live the life of your dreams."

-Oprah Winfrey

Chapter 13

My Dream

Returning to the question WHO AM I... NOW? I am still a woman who is a mother, widow, cancer survivor, former teacher, best-selling author and an entrepreneur, however I am much stronger and more confident knowing that come what may, "GOD HAS MY BACK!!"

I will continue to pivot, growing my business and evolving as an individual. My leap of faith continues, although it was greatly tested during the early part of Covid-19 when suddenly I had zero clients and zero prospects for the foreseeable future. But I adjusted my mindset and began each day with gratitude. A relentlessly positive outlook, my ability to think outside the box and no more fear-based overanalyzing all have uplifted and motivated me during these trying times.

I have handled many challenges in my life, but I have never felt as confident and at peace as I do in the present moment. I have found my Peace and Serenity, and I continue to find joy knowing I have assisted others in finding theirs. I'm a shoulder they can lean on to process emotions about items and spaces, which nearly always involve deeper issues. I'm the helping hands and feet to actively move them through the process. My eyes help shape their vision of the finished project with an outsider's fresh perspective. My sympathetic ears actively listen to their stories and concerns. And yes, sometimes I hold them in my arms when it becomes too much. I am their guide and helper for moving toward the Peace and Serenity I have found!

I'm living proof that if you dream of a different career and a different life, no matter your age or your circumstances, believe you can make it come true. It won't happen by magic and it may take longer than you'd like. Keep the faith in yourself, keep moving forward with optimism and focused effort, and you will indeed succeed in making that dream your new and wonderful reality.

www.ingramcontent.com/pod-product-compliance
Lightning Source LLC
Chambersburg PA
CBHW070938230426
43666CB00011B/2482